The People in a Girl's Life

of related interest

People Skills for Young Adults
Márianna Csóti
ISBN 1 85302 716 2

Contentious Issues
Discussion Stories for Young People
Márianna Csóti
ISBN 1 84310 033 9

The People in a Girl's Life
How to Find Them, Better Understand Them and Keep Them…

Martha Kate Downey
and Kate Noelle Downey

Jessica Kingsley Publishers
London and Philadelphia

First published in the United Kingdom in 2002
by Jessica Kingsley Publishers Ltd
116 Pentonville Road
London N1 9JB, England
and
325 Chestnut Street
Philadelphia, PA 19106, USA

www.jkp.com

Copyright © 2002 Martha Kate Downey and Kate Noelle Downey

Library of Congress Cataloging in Publication Data
A CIP catalog record for this book is available from the Library of Congress

British Library Cataloguing in Publication Data
A CIP catalogue record for this book is available from the British Library

ISBN 1 84310 707 4

Printed and Bound in Great Britain
by Athenaeum Press, Gateshead, Tyne and Wear

Contents

To our own very dear family, who taught us
about love, honor, and compassion.
And to all our Special Olympics friends,
who teach us about joy.

Acknowledgements

In 1998 a group of ladies came together as an on-line group called "Dear Daughters." The group was formed as a means of support but also to gather information and brainstorm issues to share in this book. The members of this incredibly generous group have special criteria to meet. They either have autism themselves, children with autism, or are both autistic themselves and have children sharing the diagnosis. We talk about all sorts of challenges, although our focus is on those specific to young women with neurological or developmental differences or delays. We speak honestly and freely through our computers to laugh, cry, brag and problem-solve. It has been a continued blessing to have such a resource as we help our growing daughters face new challenges. Through these years we've discovered some basic truths and I feel privileged to share them. So, to Margie Miller, Linni Paquette, Shirley Paquette, Amanda Victoria Berry, Jane Meyerding, Jean Kearns Miller, Teri, Karen Reznek, Karen Koziol, RN, Patricia M. Harkins, MD, Kalen Molton, Keri Isbell, Rochelle Hartman, Diane Wills, Karen Bradley and two wonderful editors, Jessica Kingsley and Jo Gammie, "Thank you! You're the Best! You really DO know what being a friend means!"

Love,
Martha Kate

Introduction

Hi! I'm Kate Noelle Downey. I was born in 1982. I like computers, cats and dancing. I have autism and some other challenges, just like many of you reading this book.

Because I have a harder time understanding the world and the people in it, my mom thought it would be a good idea to write down some of our conversations and share what we've learned with other Dear Daughters who have special challenges in their lives.

Hello, I'm Martha Kate Downey and Kate is my own Dear Daughter.

My husband Dennis and I are honored to be the parents of two very special children. David, our compassionate son, is now an adult. He began as a small child to teach me how to be a mom. Seven years later Kate, who is now a remarkable young woman, came along teaching me still more lessons about parenting. David and Kate are continuing their "mom training" even today.

Kate has amazing determination to enjoy her world and the people in that world. She finds people fascinating but sometimes very confusing. Through the years we've worked together to help her learn to understand the people around her. With this book, she and I hope to help other Dear Daughters learn more about living happily with their families and others in their lives. Please join us as we visit about *The People in a Girl's Life*.

Dear Daughter,

During your lifetime you will meet many, many people. Each person will be unique (no other person like them). Some of these people you will simply pass on the street, others you will take into your heart and hold close for always.

To be happy and enjoy the people we know we must learn how to get along with each of them in a comfortable way. As we go through this book we'll discover how we can adapt to the different people.

Need is one of the main reasons we have people in our lives. There is no one single person who can meet all of your needs. As you mature you will have many stages in your life. As a baby, a toddler, a girl, a teen, a young adult, a middle-ager and a retired person, you will progress and change. Your needs and wants change too. So the variety (different types) and number of people who are in your life will grow and change.

For instance, parents are in our lives to feed us, provide shelter for us and help us grow in our minds and bodies. That is my job as a mother – to take care of you. But friends have another job. They make your life more interesting and exciting. A friend's job is to share experiences with you. As you and your friends share your lives you are growing.

When you began school you added still more people to your world. Teachers and students and other workers at the school became part of your life. They all have different jobs. (That's good because no one could clean the school building, teach math, cook the food, drive the school bus, be a member on a basketball team and work in the office!) That requires your circle of people to grow quickly when you enter school.

The number of people in your life will change again when you begin a job. An employer's job is not the same as my job, your teacher's job or your friends' jobs. An employer (boss) has the job of paying you money for work that you do.

See how it works? Different people do different things for us. Some of them can help us, some cheer us on, others teach us or employ us, and some just provide fun. That's lots of jobs and that takes lots of people!

It is an important belief of mine that having many different people in the world is part of God's master plan. It seems to me that if God had intended for us to be able to do everything for ourselves, all of the time, He would have put us here on the earth one person at a time. But He didn't. He put us here in families, and groups, so we could help one another. That means I help you and you help me too!

Understanding the responsibilities we have to other people is another very important step in knowing how to get along with the people in our lives. In this book we'll talk about our responsibilities to other people and their responsibilities to us.

We'll also visit about how to become our best selves. I think you'll find that as you better understand other people you'll discover why you're a young woman who is enjoyed and treasured.

CHAPTER I

Moms and Dads, Brothers and Sisters

Dear Mom,

What is a family?

Dear Daughter,

A family is a group of people who care for one another with attention and love. Whether you have a mother, father, sister, brother, aunt, uncle or grandparents, it is important to have a family. Families become families not out of force, but by choice. Some may be blood relatives while others become your family because of the commitment you share with one another.

No matter how you got your family, the thing that makes them truly your family is the fact that you take care of one another. They are the people who have chosen to be closest to you and teach you how to grow into a happy, healthy woman. Your family will love and support you throughout your lifetime.

Hey Mom,

What is commitment and how do we show commitment to each other in our family?

Dear Daughter,

A commitment is a promise that we sometimes say out loud (like wedding vows) but many times we make vows or promises without being aware that we have.

A commitment is more than just words – it is an action, a way of thinking that says, "I will do everything in my power to keep my promises to you."

It is not always easy to live with other people. It's not easy for anyone. But when we make commitments to another person we must do everything that we can to honor those commitments. That's what makes us an "honorable" person.

You will find that the way you show commitment changes from group to group, but in our family these are our promises:

- I love you

- I respect you as a person

- I am willing to take care of you, as you do me.

We show this commitment by participating in family gatherings, listening carefully to one another and helping when we can. We also show it by accepting what a family has to offer (from advice and clean clothes to warm hugs and popcorn).

Do all parents show their love and care for each of their children in exactly the same way?

Every family will have members who need extra care or help from time to time. The responsibility of the parents is to see that everyone in the family is cared for.

Some families have a member who needs extra help or care. That means that all the family members will learn new skills to care for them. Each family member may show the care in different ways. For instance, the father might be a bit more protective of a daughter with special needs than he might be with a son who is more able to care for himself in most situations. It doesn't mean he doesn't trust her or that she is more loved. It just means that he wants to keep her from being hurt. So the type of care is adjusted to fit the needs of each family member.

Here's another example of how parents show love for children in different ways.

As a member of a Special Olympics team, you enjoy having your dad and me come to your games and activities. You, your dad and me go and enjoy cheering and coaching. It is fun for us all. But when your brother was in high school and active in sports he often did not want us coming to his events. He enjoyed the freedom of the day to go and do his own activity. He likes being independent. Therefore, we didn't go to his sports activities when he was no longer a little boy. It didn't mean that we weren't still interested – it meant that we showed our interest in different ways. We showed our interest as he needed and wanted it by asking about how his day went and making sure there was plenty of food in the house before and after his events!

You most enjoy a cheering section while he favored food and a chance to demonstrate his independence and receive our trust!

We love you both, but we show our love according to your desires and needs.

Does the way we all show commitment change with time?

Yes Kate, as a member of a family we will always help care for you. But the ways we show our commitment to you will change as your needs change and as our needs change. You'll be learning and doing more things for yourself and the family, and we will be encouraging you to take on new challenges.

As a baby you needed food, water, warmth, and touch. When you became a small child we still took care of you, but in different ways. We still touched you, but instead of only holding you as a baby in our arms we reached down to steady you as you learned to walk. It would not help a toddler learn to walk if the parent were to always carry the child.

As you practice new skills and notice things that need to be done around a house, such as carrying out the trash, cooking, or putting away laundry (without being asked), you are taking on the role of adulthood. Learning and practicing new habits lead to more independence.

But I like having people take care of me!

Oh Kate, Don't we all! But...

As human beings we get into habits. A habit is formed when our brains tell us to do the same things over and over. Sometimes habits are a very good thing – like brushing your teeth every morning. Other times habits can keep us from doing things we should. If the habit has slowed down our growth or made us lazy it is not a good habit.

You want to make sure that your habit of living is one that leads to a very rich life. Believe me, having Mom take care of you all the time would become pretty boring!

By accepting the challenge to be everything you can be, we see that you are developing into an honorable adult.

Mom,

   That word "honor." What does it mean?
Why is it important?

Dear Daughter,

Honor is what we earn by being trustworthy and honest. It is a very important thing to have because it is what makes a family strong and assures them that they can depend on one another. We show we can be trusted and are therefore honorable people by keeping promises (commitments) we make, even when we don't feel like it or when we'd rather be doing something else.

When we make promises it doesn't just mean for today. It doesn't just mean while it is easy. It means forever. That's true commitment.

Honor is important because without it we can never feel safe. We could never know if the people whom we live with could be trusted. Never knowing when something is real or not is a scary way to live. When I tell you the truth and keep my promises to you, you know that you can depend on me and that what I say is real. By showing that I am an honorable person you know that you can trust what I say and do so not just for today but for everyday.

Mom,

In our family I have, a mother, a father, a brother, grandparents and lots of other relatives. Do some of the same lessons I'm learning here apply to families that aren't quite like mine?

Yes, these lessons about dependability and responsibility apply no matter who is in your family. But each family has their own list of responsibilities and who will do those jobs. For instance, if you were the only child in our family we would have more time to spend just with you, but you might also have more chores to do around the house. Or if there is no father in the home, the mother and the children must take on some of the responsibilities that a father might share. The commitment to the family remains the same, the jobs just change.

Mom, I know that my brother has to help me with some things that other brothers don't have to do because of my differences. Is he sorry? Is his life harder because of me?

Your brother David once told me the difference in having a sister with autism versus having a sister without autism (or what some people call "normal") is like the difference between taking an easy high school course or a very difficult college course. The difficult course requires more time and forces you to work harder but it stretches your mind and takes it to new places – it helps you learn more about your world and yourself. The easier course takes much less time and thought but doesn't require you to grow or teach you new skills.

David said you are like the harder course, he feels he is now better prepared to face new challenges. Your brother believes because of the way you are he has become a stronger, better person.

Pretty smart brother, huh! He knows that easy or normal is not always best!

Is it harder for you and Daddy because I have some special challenges?

We're like your brother – we had to learn some new skills when you came along, just as we would have learned new skills with each child whether they had special challenges or not.

The important thing for you to know is that everyone in the family has special needs. We all have special challenges to face and need a family's support to accomplish them. Staying committed to one another and continuing to care for one another is not always easy but it is important. It's what keeps families together and makes us honorable people.

Getting along with brothers or sisters (siblings) may be hard to do sometimes. Do you have any special ideas that could help me do that?

You're right Kate. Getting along with brothers or sisters may require extra patience and flexibility (not always having to have things your way or the same way every time).

I think one of the hardest times siblings have getting along together is when one sibling is helping care for another, or taking them somewhere. At those times you tell us your brother may sound a little bossy to you or not let you do things that your daddy or I let you do. That is because he feels responsible for you. He doesn't want to take any chances with your being hurt or doing something that he is not sure you can do or are allowed to do. He takes his job so seriously that he almost "over parents" you.

Kind of nice to know someone loves you so much that they take too good of care of you!

But don't forget that, as a family member you also have a responsibility to care for your brother! Try these suggestions:

1.   Concentrate on the jobs to be accomplished instead of who is the boss. That way you are both thinking about something else and not just yourselves.

2.   Let everyone take care of one another. When the parent is not present, the sibling who is the safest cook would be asked to fix the meal, while the brother or sister who keeps up best with the passage of time might need to be the one to announce bed time.

No sibling will have all the needed skills. In that way we can show commitment again as a family, honor one another's skills and feel that we can all take care of one another.

Mom,

How can I make his life better?

Here are some ways we can get along with a brother
or sister who is helping us:

- Always say "Thank you!" when they have
  helped you.

- Have an agreeable spirit.

- Be fun!

- Don't argue with them in public.

- Follow their directions, even if you don't
  know why – ask about it later privately.
  They might have spotted something
  dangerous that you didn't see.

- Share with them new skills in appropriate ways, not just by arguing.

- Try to do things you know to do before they have to ask. Show your strengths by being responsible.

- Help them out, too. Remember they also need help sometimes. Do it cheerfully and what's even more fun is to do it as a surprise! It's a great way to show off new skills.

- Remember, sometimes what feels like bossiness is their way of showing they love you.

Make them glad that they had the chance to share the time with you by being pleasant and helping them out.

Pssst... You might also remember he always loves for someone else to do his laundry!

So if a family is going to be a happy one, they have to learn to work together. Right?

ℰℭ

Yes Kate, all families have struggles sometimes, but working through the difficulties will make us each stronger as individual people and the family stronger as a group.

Here are some ways we work together as a family:

1.   Placing someone else's needs ahead of our own sometimes.

2.   Realizing that each time one family member changes it affects the rest of the family too.

3.   Willingness to accept the advice or direction of someone you honor, even when you don't agree with or understand the reason for the choices they make.

4. Forgiving another person when they make a mistake.

5. Apologizing when we make a mistake and trying not to repeat the mistake again.

6. Allowing each family member to stretch and grow – in their minds as well as their bodies!

7. Respecting each other's privacy – everyone should have someplace they have no fear of being laughed at.

8. Having extra patience and being willing to do a little extra work for a family member who is under pressure, is sick or having a hard time.

Sharing information and communicating are really, really important parts of a family. For a family to decide how to work together they must all be headed in the same direction. The key to success is not in following the perfect path but in steadfastly following a path in a positive direction… together.

CHAPTER 2

CHAPTER 2

Other Relatives

Mom,

How about all those other relatives? They are all so different, and so many of them. Do I have to change me to get along with each of them?

Dear Daughter,

Many families have brothers, sisters, mothers, fathers, aunts, uncles, grandparents and cousins. Some families have god parents or step-family members too. That can be a lot of people!

Managing to get along with all those types of relatives is not easy for any of us. How well we get along with them is often a matter of our commitment to share our lives with them.

Different family members need different things. A cousin might need a playmate while a grandparent might need a warm hug or a nice smile. (Grandparents like telephone calls too, but not too long a conversation.)

Learning to adjust how you are with a relative is the same as learning to adjust how you behave with different friends. Some want to hear every part of your day, while others only want to know whether or not you went to school. It is not always easy to know exactly how much a person wants to hear so give your information in brief pieces, letting them have the opportunity to ask questions if they want to know more or share information about their lives too.

One thing I think is true is that people who know and understand us will be more comfortable sharing their lives with us.

You are a daughter who comes in a little "different flavor" (extra spicy with a touch of autism for added zest). As your mother, over the years I have tried to help the rest of the family understand some of your mannerisms, thoughts and activities. The more your cousins learned, the more you became involved with their lives and they involved with yours. You cheer for their college teams and they come watch your Special Olympics games.

It is hard for a relative to show commitment to you if you haven't shared important things about your life. It doesn't mean they don't care, it just shows that they don't know you well enough to be very involved.

Share your life and they'll be more likely to share theirs too. And remember to show as much enthusiasm for them and their interests as they do for you. Send cards, call and ask about their lives when you're with them. Help them when they need help. True commitment goes both ways!

Hey Mom,

Some of my relatives treat me as a favorite. I just want to be one of the kids! (Okay, sometimes I like to be the special one, but everyone does!) What's the deal? What do I do about that?

Dear Daughter,

Your aunts, uncles or grandparents don't mean to be treating you as a favorite (you know that if they do it makes the other children feel less important). Sometimes they give you more attention because you might need it. If you're in a wheelchair you need help getting up and down stairs or in and out of cars. You *do* need more help sometimes, but thanking them and then turning the attention onto others is a good way to help everyone feel their share of the love.

Some grandparents feel guilty about your special challenges, especially if it is genetic, and for those reasons they may not respond the same way to you as they do to other grandchildren. Letting them know that you are happy lets them begin to see you in a more "normal" way and treat you more as they do the other grandchildren.

**Not every relative treats me the same way.
Why is that?**

Some people, not just relatives, simply don't "get it." They don't understand how or why you need more help than they do, or than they did at your age. Sometimes people (even family members) can act angry with you because they are afraid they don't know how to help you or talk to you, while others may just not want to be close to all the members of their family.

Just like all people you meet, some relatives will be close to you and others will not. They are each individuals and even though they have come from the same family their approach to life may be quite different. Learn to embrace the relatives that are the most comfortable with you and let the others go on to other things in their lives. Who knows, someday they might become closer to you because they better understand you or have realized they need your help and support.

Mom, sometimes they leave me out...

Sometimes we're all left out...

But that makes me remember an important thought. Even though you might feel that you are the only one that gets left out of activities, or is treated unkindly, if you'll look around you'll see that it generally isn't just you who is being left out or ignored. They are likely to be ignoring or leaving out others as well.

Be generous with your thoughts. Realize that the reason they are leaving you out may have nothing to do with you. They may be having a bad day. They may not know quite how to include you or they may simply be overwhelmed with the number of people around them. (Especially if it is a holiday family gathering.) Remember, sometimes you want to be alone too, and that's okay.

Hey Mom,

What about the times when I seem to irritate my relatives? I don't mean to bother them or make them nervous. What do I do about that?

Dear Kate,

Sometimes everyone gets irritated. Even best of friends can get too much of one another. If another person begins to act as though you are irritating them (bothering them with questions, talk or habits) you might try giving them a break. You can tell when they need a break by watching to see:

- how interested they are in a game
- do they look at you
- if their voice is getting higher
- and if they are anxious to finish the conversation or game.

If you sense irritation you might try changing some things about your next visit. Next time when you are planning to be with them allow for some breaks apart. Only play a game or two with them, then take a break for awhile (an hour or so) and do something with someone else or by yourself. Remember you're good company for yourself! Have them anxious to see you and to be with you, without worrying that you might wear them out.

You know I'm getting older and stronger and more capable. Guess it would be nice to help them as they have helped me?

Great idea Kate!

Make them look forward to your visits because they can see your commitment to them too. Find ways to make their lives easier. See how you can help them out when you are with them. Carrying out the trash, helping in the kitchen, walking the dog and raking the yard are all things that save them a little energy (something they have less of and you probably have more of). In other words, use your strengths to help with their weaknesses, because that's what a strong family does.

Love,

Mom

CHAPTER 3

Family and Beyond

I've noticed that some families need help.
Do all families need help sometimes?

Yes they do. Everyone has times in his or her lives that are difficult. Sometimes groups of people (like a whole family) need help to work together or understand one another. Other times one person may need some extra help. What is important to remember is that getting help is a smart thing to do. It doesn't show weakness. It shows that you are working to be the best you can be.

There are many places to find help and many different types of help are available. There are programs, support groups and counselors within agencies and schools, religious places (such as churches and synagogues, etc). They are there just to help you. If you are a young woman who needs help understanding your feelings, protecting yourself from someone hurting you, help with school work or maybe finding a job, there are people in your community who can help you. They help with other kinds of problems too.

Hey Mom,

What if I need more people in my life that are close to me and care about me as my family? Is that okay? How do I find these people?

Dear Daughter,

Families come in many different ways. Some of us are physically born into families who are prepared to care for and nurture us (feed our bodies, our minds and our spirits). Others find their true families in other places.

A parent is a person who chooses to commit her or his attention, resources (time and money and energy) toward helping another person grow into a healthy, productive person. We can find parents in many ways. If you grew within your mother's body then she was your biological mother. If something happens and that woman cannot be a parent then you need to find a mother in other ways. Some of the

Dear Daughters reading this book have been adopted, like you were Kate. Some found mothers early in life, some much later. Usually, we can find those women and men who care about us in our extended families, our schools, religious institutions (such as churches, synagogues, etc) or neighbor-hoods.

I hope you will have the joy of knowing many caring people throughout your lifetime. People who will love you and nurture you. The important thing to understand is in order to grow we must have nurturing. And if that nurturing is not readily found in the place where you are living, it is appropriate and healthy for you to seek out a person with whom you can share your life and interests. Someone who can help you grow, learn new skills and provide a role model (a person who does something in a way that you would like to learn). This is a common way to find comfort.

Hey Mom,

What if I already have lots of family members who support me and love me but can't always answer some of my questions about my disability? What do I do when I need to talk to someone who really knows how I feel?

Dear Daughter,

For many reasons, families can sometimes provide some of the nurturing needed, but not all.

It is hard for me to know what it would be like to have autism. Even though I know many people with that diagnosis, I can not truly know how they feel about having the disability. It is often helpful then for the daughter growing up with autism, Down Syndrome or any other difference to find another person who has the same thing. They can share their ideas and feelings. They may help each other grow. That is an example of how we can have other people who also teach and nurture us as parents do.

Wouldn't that hurt your feelings?

No Kate, it wouldn't hurt my feelings. In fact, I feel better when I know you are getting all the help you need, not just the help I can provide. All of us need people who understand our particular needs. It is okay to seek that.

For Dear Daughters who are looking for a special person who shares their special needs here are a few suggestions:

- Make it clear to your family that you still love them and are committed to your family, but explain that because you have some different challenges than they have it would be helpful to share those thoughts or feelings with a person who shares your syndrome or exceptional needs.

- Let your family know that their helping you find a special person is another way they care for you.

- If you don't already know someone who shares your challenges, ask a trusted person such as your mother, teacher or neighbor to help you find a special friend who can provide understanding.

- Realize seeking help and understanding is a very healthy, smart thing to do!

Hey Mom,

I wish I had a sister. And sometimes as I get older and I am more on my own I find I need a person to help me better understand problems in my life. It's sort of like needing another mother.

Just as we find people to help nurture us, like a parent, it is also okay to find people to share our lives in other ways. I had two brothers but no sisters. I needed to have a girl with whom I could share "girl stuff" in my life. To make up for never having sisters, I found a girl my age in my neighborhood – she and I came to be such friends that we were almost like sisters. Later I met other girls and women who cared about my life and whose lives I cared about. We continue to share thoughts and feelings that my brothers would find most uninteresting. I have always found it important to have someone nearby who shares my life as a sister would. In this way I "choose" sisters.

We also all need help in making decisions in our lives and having a special friend or two to help and listen with a caring ear is very important. It will be important throughout your lifetime. As we all get older you may not always live in the house with your father and me. You may not see us as often. In those cases it is helpful to find another person who you see more often to help guide you in your life. When you are grown you'll find that sometimes someone younger than yourself might even act as a guide for you. Age isn't important – the wisdom the person has and the commitment you have for each other is what counts!

Love,
Mom

p.s. Anyone you choose as a family member is a very lucky person Kate!

CHAPTER 4

Friends, Boyfriends, Life-long Friends and Husbands

Mom, please teach me about making friends.

Dear Daughter,

You'll meet thousands of people during your lifetime. They are each unique (no one else like them). Some of these people you will just pass on the street, others you will learn to know well and care for. Most of the people will be ones with whom you share only portions of your life. Finding those individuals who will become friends is a fun thing to do, but one we must do carefully and wisely.

Strangers are people whom we do not know. Sometimes they will become a friend, but sometimes we need to stay out of their way and avoid them.

That's why it is important that if we choose to include a person in our lives, we slowly and carefully examine them to see if they are honorable, caring people. Here are the steps we take to do that:

- When we meet a new person, normally we first notice how that person looks, dresses or speaks. We see the outside of who they are; the things they allow everyone to see.

- If the person makes you nervous then I would avoid them until you were assured by another trusted friend that they were safe people to know. That's why we often make friends through introductions from other friends. It is a better way to meet a new person than simply by striking up a conversation on a bus, or while standing in line at the store. Introductions are our way of saying, "Here is a friend of mine. You can trust him or her." It gives you more information than you can gather from just watching or talking with someone.

- Outside clues don't tell us if someone will make a good friend. They might have a closet full of "cool" clothes or a smile on their face, but little warmth and caring in their heart.

So I can't tell by just looking at them whether or not they will become a good friend or not?

That's correct Kate – first comes a bit of detective work.

No matter how, when or where you meet a person first, the beginnings are all the same. You meet the person then, after the first introduction, you begin to explore (look at) ways you and the person are alike and different. As you find out the things they like to do, watch their actions, listen to the way they speak about others and discover more of their personality, you move from seeing the outside of them to knowing the inside of them.

Next think how you feel about what you've learned. Sometimes the ways you are alike will delight you. You will think it is fun that you share an idea, a feeling or a hobby. You might feel comfortable with them because you understand the other person well. Other times the new person might be so much like you that they bore you. They may always say things that you already know.

In general, we find new things interesting. We want to know more about them. We might be seeing "old" ideas in a new way, through another person's eyes and mind. This new look may be exciting. It can be fun to meet people who have had different experiences and thoughts.

Whether a person is like you or not like you, you will need to make sure your life is better with them – not just *different* – before deciding if they are to be a trusted friend.

Mom,

Sometimes I meet people who act as if they want to be my friend, but they confuse me. They ask me to do something that people I trust never ask me to do. How can I tell whether or not a person is trying to trick me and just pretending to be my friend?

Some people you meet (for example, total strangers, casual acquaintances or family friends) will act friendly (by smiling and chatting with you) but ask you to do some things that you know are not a good idea.

These people are NOT friends at all!

They pretend they are good friends of yours (by acting friendly, appearing to be interested in your life, your family, etc) because they want to take something from you. Sometimes it is money. They might try selling you something you don't need or that could hurt you (like drugs or alcohol). They might also try to sell you something that might not work, like a broken watch or car. They might try to borrow money from you (more than $5.00) or ask you to keep a secret about something you know is wrong. Beware – these people are only pretending to be your friends.

A real friend will not try to steal from you or get you into trouble! They will not want you to hurt your mind, your body or your reputation (what people think they know about you) in any way. They will *not* ask you to lie.

If the information they give you is very different from the information you already know to be good and true and healthy *do not trust them*. They have a reason to talk you into bad habits. And it is not a good reason for you!

Dear Mom,

Are there different kinds of friends?

Yes there are lots of different kinds of friends, just as there are different members of a family. Family members, employers and co-workers may all become friends. But not every employer or co-worker will become a close personal friend.

Some of the people you know will become very important to you. You will want to share much information about yourself with them. Other people you meet may be people you only see occasionally, people who share some interests with you but who don't care about the same things you care about. You may enjoy their company at work or at a club meeting but decide not to spend other time with them. These are casual friends.

A casual friend is like an acquaintance – someone that is in your life but doesn't share the important parts of your life with you. That does not mean that they are bad friends but they are not ones you would trust with your most special thoughts. They might not respond to you in as friendly a way. Or they may not reciprocate favors. They might not choose to hurt you but you find that sometimes they do hurt you because they don't care for and value the same things as you do. Those people might share part of your life but you will not choose to share the most private parts of your heart.

I've heard you use the word "reciprocal" before. Sometimes you say we need to "reciprocate the favor." What do those words mean?

If you're always the one to call, or make the effort to include another person then that friendship may not be a "reciprocal" friendship.

Reciprocity means that you each give and take in the friendship. You call them and they call you. That is an important part of friendship. Otherwise, they may be "nice people" but not ones who truly enjoy you. And good friends really enjoy one another. Each needs the other.

It is okay to have people you know who don't reciprocate. Perhaps they call you often but you don't like to call them. Unless they are trying to hurt you, then it is wisest to be kind to them but don't promise things you don't intend to do.

In the same manner, sometimes you will be more interested in another person than they are in you. That doesn't mean either of you are "bad" people, or bad friends, it just means that the friendship only shares certain areas of interest. You will find this happens sometimes at work, school or other places where you have more casual friendships.

I sort of go by a three-turn rule. If I have contacted them first on three different occasions and they have not reciprocated by calling me, I move on to someone else. I might be interested in them but for some reason they are not choosing to become a closer friend of mine. It's okay! We all like to have the freedom to pick our friends.

If I am interested in getting to know someone at work or school better, how do I do that?

Try sharing a little more personal information about yourself, but be sure it is something that you wouldn't mind if anyone else knew (just in case they prove to be a person who gossips).

You might ask a question or two about something they have mentioned in their own lives. If they answer your questions in a friendly way (smiling and looking at you), then go on to ask you more questions, then you'll know you're on your way to a closer friendship.

When's the best time and place to do that?
I know at the workplace I stay on task and
work!

That's true Kate. You have to be careful that you don't let your social life get in the way of your doing a good job!

In general, during lunch or break is a good time to visit about more personal things. If you enjoyed your casual conversations during lunchtime or breaks and would like to spend more time with them you might suggest meeting again, perhaps outside the school or work place. Watching a movie or playing a game are good ways to share time together and collect more information about another person. In general it is easier to make conversation if there is something to do or watch because it provides something to talk about. Attending an exhibit about your shared interest or participating in a sport that you both enjoy is fun too.

It is very important that you choose places that are safe ones when you are getting to know someone. Meet in public places where you could get help if you need it. (Just in case the person doesn't turn out to be as nice as you thought they were.)

If a person shares information that is scary or confusing, or does something to me that is inappropriate (like touching my breasts or hitting me), what do I do?

If a person tells you something that scares you or you discover that they intend to hurt themselves or someone else, then that is information that you must share with a person you trust and with people in charge.

If possible, first discuss the matter with a person you know and trust (a family member or close friend). Then you must tell someone of authority (a person in charge). At work it would be your boss or another person with authority. At school you would tell your teacher, counselor and school principal. That way you'll know that several people will be on the lookout for dangerous behavior. Everyone you tell should be told confidentially (that means you don't gossip or tell anyone who does not need to know).

Be aware that the person who wants to hurt someone may be angry that you told his or her secret. However, you should keep in mind that you are not breaking a friendship but making the effort to keep someone safe. Safety of yourself and others is more important than the fact that a person may be angry. If the person told you they were considering hurting you, themselves or someone else, you would not only tell the school or work authorities but also possibly the police.

It is always good to continue to talk to the person whom you know well and trust. They can help you decide who and what to tell and also help you understand your scary or confused feelings.

Do we trust everyone in the same way?

No, you'll find that different people have different abilities and skills. You might trust them one way but not in another. For example, if a friend did not have a good memory and often forgets important meetings I would not depend on that friend for a ride to work but I might trust the friend in other ways. If that same person is a good decision-maker, listener and never breaks a confidence (by telling your private information), I would trust them to discuss an important question. Every person has different skills. I trust this person in some areas, but not all.

The best way to learn how dependable they are is in a gradual way. This is a very important thing to remember. Do not trust a person for something very, very important unless you have already had experience in knowing their skills and caring in that area. It would be like jumping in the deep end of a swimming pool before finding out if the water was safe. When swimming, first you put in your toe to see how cold the water is, then your foot. You check to see how deep it is, you might even ask the lifeguard if it is safe. We check out strangers (new people) and situations in the same way – a little at a time. We don't dive into marriage or a sexual relationship without knowing the safety and life commitment that is there with the new person. Get a good history before you trust and trust only in areas where you know they can deliver.

Uh Mom,

What about boyfriends or someone I might want to marry or have as a close life-long friend? How do I choose them?

Dear Daughter,

A boyfriend or close friend starts out first as a regular friend. If he or she becomes an important friend in your life, one that makes you happy, helps you make good decisions and live a happy safe life, then they will very likely make a good life-long friend. It is important to have long-term friendships whether we marry or not.

Just remember – a good friend you choose as a life-mate will share your values (those things that are important to you). If he or she doesn't care about and honor the same things, they may make an okay friend but not one you might choose for a close friend and certainly not someone you might consider marrying.

Here are some things you might consider when deciding if a person is to be a life-mate:

1. **Is the other person kind to you, their parents and other people?**

2. **Are the people in their lives important to them?** Would the person put their family's needs before their own enjoyment or leisure time?

3. **Are they honest?** Remember, if they lie to another person they will probably lie to you.

4. **Do they keep their promises?** Can you trust them to do the things they promise to do? Can you know for sure that if they promise to be your friend, team-mate or date, that they will keep their promise – even if something more fun comes up? (There are some reasons that are okay to break a promise, for example a doctor's appointment or car problems. Do they let you know ahead of time, if possible?)

5. **Could you trust them with your most important thing – your life?**

6. **Do they honor your privacy?** Are they respectful of confidential information or your need to be alone sometimes?

7. **Do you both share a common faith?** Do you understand and honor the friend's beliefs about God, or church, etc?

8. **Do you both value your time together?** Is the other person glad to see you? Are they excited and happy to greet you when you visit or call? Do they also call and pay visits to you or are you always the person who makes the contact?

Dear Daughter,

Take care in choosing your friends. Know that being a good friend is a good way to finding a good friend.

Love,

Mom

CHAPTER 5

People in Public Places

Mom,

What about people at the grocery store, school, work, etc? What do I say to them? How do I know what to do? I know that I wouldn't do the same things in a jewelry store that I do in a grocery store. I also know that at a football game it is okay to talk loudly, but not in a library. Help!

Dear Daughter,

Learning how to manage in public is a very tricky thing to do. Just about the time you learn what is appropriate to do and say in one place, we go somewhere else and there are different things you say and do.

Here are a few basic ideas:

1. **Watch the other people in the place.** Are they chatting or listening to the music or a speaker? Are they using quiet voices? Are they remaining in one place or standing in a line? How do they go about getting the services they need? Are they standing in a line until they are called (like at the post office)? Are they all looking straight ahead, with no conversation?

2. **Have your money ready when it is needed.** For example, when you buy tickets for a movie or pay for food at a fast food place.

3. **Try to go with a person you trust the first time you're in a new situation.** Ask them for hints about what to expect and how to act. Most people do that when preparing for a new experience.

Hey Mom,

How do I know what to say or how much to say when visiting with a person?

If they are chatting, are they taking turns doing that? How long are their conversations? In general, if you are with a person who is trying to work (the checker at a store, a clerk in the post office, a receptionist) a brief pleasant comment is all that is necessary. "The weather is certainly cold" or, "It is busy in here today" or simply, "How are you?" are good comments. If they seem to want to chat that is okay. But make sure you are not slowing down their job progress, especially if there is a line of people waiting for help. If it is someone you know and no one else is waiting, a slightly longer chat is okay.

In general conversation sometimes we have a tendency to want to give lots of information to another person, but not take in their information or hear about their interests as well. That is true especially if you are young, but as we get older we realize that a conversation must be fun for others to want to have one with us.

So, a good way to learn how to act is by watching other people. Does that mean I should always copy what other people do and say?

Watching and mimicking others can help us become more comfortable and able to function more easily in groups. However, it is *not* necessary that you be like everyone else all of the time, especially if everyone else is making poor choices (like smoking, etc). It just means that by matching general behaviors in a crowd you will be safer and less vulnerable because you will not be so easily noticed.

Mom,

What does that word "vulnerable" mean?

That's a big word for a very scary instance. "Vulnerable" describes a time when we are without our protection. If you were out in the cold weather without a coat you would be vulnerable to the cold. If you were walking alone at night on a dark city street you would appear to be vulnerable to someone who might be looking for trouble or someone to steal from or hurt.

Most parents and siblings don't want you to appear to be vulnerable in public. They worry that you might be spotted as someone needing more care and think that they could hurt you more easily than they might someone who looked more alert or stronger. They might not want you to handle your money in public, afraid that if someone knew it was difficult for you to make change they might be more likely to give you the wrong amount of money when they made your change, or not give you change at all. They might charge you more than the usual amount or tell you something untrue about your ticket. That is a way a person might take advantage of you.

Is that why my brother seems bossier to me when we are in public together? Or am I just more sensitive at those times?

Dear Daughter,

There are times when your brother or sister may give you more directions than usual. If you are in a public place or new place your brother usually gives you more directions than he does if you are just going for a ride or playing a game at home. That is because he feels responsible for you. At home he can better control who else is there and what will happen while you are at home. But when you go out in public there are more people there and he knows that he cannot control the other people or what will happen while you are out. For those reasons he is a little more nervous about keeping you safe and might treat you a little younger than he usually does. Just relax – it just shows he cares. And after you're back in the car or in a safer place, tell him how you felt or what you think. Sometimes he may not be aware of what he is doing or that it makes you uncomfortable.

Sometimes the world is just too full of people and I need to be left alone. Is that rude?

Oh Kate,

When you feel like that, take a break. We all need breaks from people sometimes. It's okay – it's healthy to be alone at times.

Remember that you are also an important person. Leave time for you to enjoy that very special person – yourself!

For many girls like you Kate, the circle of family and friends broadens (gets larger) as they become more independent and they find that they enjoy meeting a wider variety of people. Other girls may prefer only having a small group of people in their lives. As long as your body and mind and spirit are happy and healthy, the number of people you see each day is not important. But the way they treat you and make you feel is *very* important! And the way you remember to help care for others is also *very* important!

Love,

Mom

CHAPTER 6

You! Being Your Very Best Self

Mom,

I want to be the very best person I can be. I know that means being honorable. Sometimes things happen and I'm not sure what I should do. What do I do when a person I thought was a good friend says or does something that really, really hurts my feelings?

You are right – it does hurt when someone you thought was a friend lets you down. That can happen for several reasons though. A good friend like you are will think about all the reasons the misunderstanding might have happened before deciding to get angry or hurt her friend in return.

Sometimes the person is just having a bad day. Something in their life might have hurt them and they needed a friend. You might see if that is the case and ask them if they are okay. Having a friend who cares can make a big difference in the things that we say or do.

Sometimes what we heard was not what was said or what they intended to say. This happens too often when we believe something that someone else told us they heard. It gets less believable every time it is repeated. If you didn't hear it for yourself don't believe a negative thing about another person (especially if the person has been a long-term and trusted friend). Trust your history with the friend before you trust gossip.

By the way Kate, a person who is honorable will still make mistakes from time to time, but if they have always tried to be honest and showed commitment to you in the past then you know that they are doing their best. You know that when they make mistakes it is not because they don't care about you but is simply because sometimes we all make mistakes, have misunderstandings or forget things.

I guess that means that to be my best self
I must remain committed to my friends and
family.

Yes Kate. Remaining committed to your family and friends is an important other way you show your best self.

To get along in families and with other people too, we must be able to forgive mistakes. The honorable person who has made a mistake will admit the mistake and show they are sorry. They prove they are sorry by learning from their mistakes and making every effort not to make that mistake again. Otherwise "I'm sorry" is just a meaningless phrase.

This is a hard question, but one I worry about. Am I a bad person if I decide I can't trust someone?

Kate, being a wise person does not make you a "bad person" or a dishonorable person. Sometimes we have to make decisions that make us unhappy but keep us safe.

If a person continually lets us down and doesn't keep their promises to others or to us, we will need to remember to protect ourselves by not counting on that person for important things.

I have a theory – I choose to honor the honorable. If you act responsibly and in a caring manner, I will trust you. But if you choose to live in a dishonorable way by hurting or lying to others or to me over and over, I still may care about you but will not choose to depend on you for important things.

Kate, that's why it is so important that you always be honorable, tell the truth and keep your promises. It takes a long time for a person to rebuild trust between two people when it is broken. Trust and honor can be earned again but it takes a long time if they had begun a habit of lying frequently. Just be honest. It is much easier to always be truthful and never lose your friends trust in the first place.

Mom,

Sometimes I think I'm telling the truth but what I say is not accurate. It is hard for me to know the difference between opinion and fact. It is also hard for me to know if I understand the facts I've heard. Help!

One important thing to think about when you are giving information is the problem of fact versus opinion or your understanding of the facts. Sometimes you will say things you think are true but are not accurate. You are not lying but people might think you are. If you will learn to put phrases such as, "It might be…" or, "I think that…" or, "Perhaps," or, "Could it be…", then the listener will know that you are telling something as you understand it. It helps people trust you.

Hey, Mom,

How do I fit in but still be "me?"

We've talked so much about how to avoid being noticed in a crowd but, actually, being noticed is fine if you are noticed for the right reasons. You don't want to worry so much about being just like other people that you lose your own strong talents and gifts or the courage to stand up for something good when the group around you is making a poor choice.

I love to watch, read and learn about other people. Is that a good thing to do?

Yes, it is a very good thing. We can find people that way who will inspire us to be great people ourselves. By studying those people we can learn ways to do that. We might also learn lessons from examples of people who have made poor choices in their lives. I usually find it much more fun to read about those that I admire.

Sometimes a person we notice may have some things we would like to copy but other things we might not want to copy. If you hear a singer you like, you might like the sound of her voice but don't like the words to the songs she sings. Choose the best – enjoy the melody but make better choices for lyrics. Choose the best and then let the rest go on by.

Remember, no matter how much you admire someone else you must still be who you are, the best that you are. Don't try to become someone else because the world would be poorer without your own special gifts.

Does the way that I dress and treat other people cause them to think of me differently? Is what I wear really so important?

What you wear really doesn't say who you are but it does affect who people *think* you are! Remember at the beginning of the book where we said the first thing you notice about a person is the way they are dressed? Then you notice the way they act.

How you dress and act give people the first clues about you. If you choose to wear clothing that shows lots of your body, don't be surprised if other people think that you place high value on how you look or on drawing attention to yourself. Don't dress in a way that draws attention away from the very best part of yourself – your heart and your mind. You want them to notice your kindness and your sense of humor, not just the way you dress. If you look clean and alert, they will see a person who cares that they are pleasant to be around.

How you act tells people about you too. If you appear to be bored they will probably notice that too, and they might decide that they wouldn't visit with you because you might find them boring. But if you have a pleasant look on your face and greet them in a friendly manner they will be more likely to be friendly to you, too. See what I mean? Show the type of person you are! It makes a big difference in the type of people who will want to meet you.

Remember – the way you behave causes the people around you to react to you in similar ways.

So dressing in a neat and clean way and smiling pleasantly makes people want to know me. What other ways can I encourage people who are also honorable to want to know me better?

The best way to encourage a person is by being interested in them, asking questions and listening carefully to their answers. Be careful that your questions are not too personal (like asking their age). An easy way to do that is to follow up with questions about things they have already mentioned.

Watch your general manners too. If you're at a party it is good to notice lots of things. How much you put on a plate, how your face looks as you are eating, (take a mirror with you or ask a friend to check your face after you eat if necessary) are things you need to be careful about. Do you use a napkin? If you bump someone do you apologize? Be courteous to others.

Do you invite others to share their lives, or are you only interested in giving information about yourself? This is true at other places than just parties. At church, school, sports events or practices, the coaches and teachers are also people. It pleases them when you care about them too. As you get older, you should begin to relate to them as an adult. You should begin to watch for ways that you may help them, even nurture (take care of and encourage) them. Adult caregivers have lives too. If you want to have a friend, you must be one.

Mom, am I a good friend?

Yes Kate, you are a very good friend. Here are some reasons why:

- You rejoice with your friends when something wonderful happens to either of you and grieve with one another about things that make you sad.

- You are honest, but never cruel, jealous or rude when your friend gains something you would also treasure.

- You don't tease your friends about boyfriends or break confidences – unless the secret you promised to keep is not a safe one for your friend or someone else.

- You believe in your friends and encourage them in their dreams. You show confidence in them as people. That is very important. Everyone needs a personal cheerleader. You do that well!

- You share what you have from movies to books, but perhaps the most generous and proving way of all is you'll share your very last, very delicious, chocolate chip cookie with another very good friend!

Dear Mom,

Thanks for the help. That's a lot of information. Do you mind putting it all together for me?

I'll try Kate.

1. Know your own values and do the things that make you be the best person you can be.

2. Be committed to those you love.

3. Be honest.

4. Care about others and try to understand them.

5. When you make mistakes, apologize. Try not to make them again.

6. Have a forgiving nature, but choose whom you trust wisely.

7. Be willing to try new ideas and activities, but make sure they fit in with the best you.

8. Don't tease about sensitive things (matters that are private or very important to the person).

9. Believe in yourself. Have confidence.

10. Look for the best in people.

11. Trust your instincts (those unexplained feelings we have about right or wrong).

12. Make sure you give as much in relationships as you get.

13. Make it a personal, life-long goal to leave the world a little better place because you lived.

To all the Dear Daughters reading this book,

If there are questions you have that are not answered in this book please ask a trusted friend or family member. Remember every question you ask is important. It's a fun way for you to learn about the people in your life.

Take care,
Kate and Mom